I0099425

Family Matters

Poems by

JP DiBlasi

BLUE LIGHT PRESS ❖ 1ST WORLD PUBLISHING

1st WORLD
PUBLISHING

SAN FRANCISCO ❖ FAIRFIELD ❖ DELHI

Family Matters

1ST WORLD LIBRARY
PO Box 2211
Fairfield, IA 52556
www.1stworldpublishing.com

BLUE LIGHT PRESS
www.bluelightpress.com
bluelightpress@aol.com

BOOK & COVER DESIGN
Melanie Gendron
melaniegendron999@gmail.com

AUTHOR PHOTO
JP DiBlasi

FIRST EDITION

ISBN: 978-1-4218-3580-8

For My Brother, Robert
a frequent partner in crime

Contents

April

I await the blooming of lilacs
old shoots dug by my father
from his father's garden
later planted in mine

I don't minimize
the glory of morning glories
the yellows of forsythia
the whites of snow drops
awakening among the rocks
without prodding or dare

But the lilacs –
maybe it's the gentle
nudging of earth
a transplanting of roots
or resettlement of generations

Easter Sunday

I carry the tradition of visiting graves
small memorials
carved with family names

I leave palm crosses
textured stones of surprise
and shiny unspent pennies
tokens of love and remembrance

Today I walked this ritual alone
a task assigned to me
before my birth

Figs

In the tunnel of my dreams
that I enter through doorless sleep
memories hang in unanchored suspension
faded and gray
blue as arctic ice

succulent as the figs on the trees
my grandfather brought from Sicily
always out of my reach
but never out of my dreams

Inheritance

It was a single
chocolate chip cookie
crisp on the edges
soft in the middle
set on a golden
iridescent carnival glass
plate.

It had been removed by my brother,
from its layered stash
each separated by wax paper
upon his discovery of the large round tin
painted with pastel-colored flowers,
in the back of the freezer.

This is our inheritance,
my brother said.
We were always mother's fortune.

The Coat

The honey satin lining
feels cool against my skin
as I slip inside,
burying my arms
in my mother's empty sleeves
soon to warm me,
envelope me in her touch.

I remember as a child –
her arms around my shoulders
drawing me near.

I breathe the faint remains
of her favorite perfume,
listen to rustled memories
of her evening dress as it whispers
her entrance into the room,
filling it with the silence
of only her presence.

I close my eyes and soon become her,
the one who holds me,
twists a lock of my hair
around her finger
and tells me she loves me,
that I'm her moon-faced
best girl.

Daddy Joe

For My Dad

They called him spaghetti head,
tomato face, olive skin boy,
garlic breath, black hand,
crazy Mussolini man.

But when he swung his bat,
careening that ball into the left field bleachers,
they jumped to their feet.

As he rounded the bases,
closing on home,
he became Joe, Joe,
our man Joe.

My Brother's Summer Shirts

I'm putting away your summer shirts,
now a bit too large.
Each short sleeved with collar,
no logo on the chest.

I spread soft blue haze on the bed,
smooth the fabric like I'm caressing your back
and align the sleeves before folding it in thirds.
I fold teal shadow, spiced apricot, golden candlelight.

I fasten the top button so each collar lies flat,
a still life painting in your dresser drawer,
the hint of spice sachet, enough to wonder
if they will see the coming summer sun.

Postscripts

Today I'm shredding you:
worn calendars of medical appointments
lists of prescriptions
some too difficult to pronounce
directives of what to swallow
at the exact time of day
instructions of what to eat
and what to avoid.

Pages of insurance claims
billing codes
covered costs
the burden of claim denials
& copayment balances.

Then I realize you're
risen from this bondage
in the infinite light of heaven's galaxies
singing alleluias in the celestial choir.

Fathers and Sons

"The dead are not under the earth"
– Sweet Honey in the Rock

Walking the once snow-covered ghost path
son following father
their footprints slip perfectly
into the petrified impressions
walked by those before them

Another generation's winter
lost to spring's promises
the exodus of ice
stone flies and midges
skimming cold water
food for rainbows

Blue faces of wood anemones
a sacred sign whispered in stories
from father to son
about their home far away

Day of the Dead

*The Day of the Dead celebrates the belief that the spirits
of the deceased return to the land of the living*

Will there be a cold blue wind
this evening when the families of those who died
this year gather to remember?

The night will crackle in the womb of space
I'll bring your photo into the gauzy stillness of the church.
I bought a new satin black frame – there's a thin gold line
along the inner edge.

It better shows your kind face
I'll speak your name for prayers
in the procession of souls.

I know you'll be there to hear me

Reunion

Eleven months after my brother died
I'm standing at the water's edge
in the same sandy patch by the lake
where we filled our small red pails
with shovels of rough sand castle hope.

I search the sky for his face
in the cumulus clouds of the Vermont sky
hoping to see his smile in the fluffy white
of shape shifting puppy dogs
imperfectly matched angel wings
and the horse with the huge white mane.

Today I don't find him
but I know
he's playing hide and seek.

Whisper of the Trees

"The stories only trees can tell" – Prartho Sereno

I wasn't really lost
as much as looking for that place I knew
until the last person who loved me died.

I've visited old haunts
creaky docks
wood piles
now cathedrals to mice
leaky rowboats soon to be pulled
out of baptism's water
upside down for the winter
a bit like me.

Reflected in the lake
I see the time I fell over backward
off the dock
trying to pull you up
out of the water
laughing then, remembering now.

Last autumn's pilgrimage I walked
through hooded columns of white birches
breathing in the incense of pines at vespers
and heard a celestial choir of trees
whisper my name
as if they knew me.

Night Song

I go to the lake of loons
to its cold baptismal water
for atonement or anointment

That place where loons
like chanting monks
confer forgiveness
without necessary
penance or blame

A journey of return
from the other side of darkness.

The Deer

Friday's dusk draped over my small patch
of unmanicured grass and flowers
in the honey-colored tones
of the old masters

I lingered in the beauty
long enough to see a young deer
in its reddish-brown coat
standing in front of the stone wall
its head turned toward me
its black eyes staring through mine

As the colors of the old masters darkened
the deer lowered its front legs
as if to kneel in prayer
and sat down while looking at me
as I looked back into
familiar black eyes.

Sanctuary

As evening approaches
its hushed light fades into the horizon
fracturing the spectrum
of white light
that ignites the sky.

I close the curtains
restoring each room's privacy
carefully leaving a slivered opening
between the folds,
a safe home for darkness
long before it was mine.

Offerings of Each Day

In the spin of its axis
the universe bestows the will of its day
gauzy golden light at sunrise
the Fahrenheit of sun
its sting of wind in my face

In the architecture of clouds
I see in white and gray
images sketched in my dreams

The phosphorescence of sunsets
never quite lingering long enough
for me to hear its sizzle

But in the unfathomable darkness of space
beyond the zenith of thought
I see a revelation of heaven

Nowhere and Everywhere

The saddle is not new to me
smooth mahogany leather
worn dark reins leading
from an iron bit in a pony's mouth
into my small hands

Three times around the dusty ring
on those cloudless Saturday afternoons
seemingly going nowhere yet everywhere

All at once
and forever
every time I think
the journey's ended

Day for a Kite

At the sharp edge of dawn
when day and night are one
the voice of silence
whispers *wake up*
rise through the veil
of morning's ochre haze

Bluest of blue crocuses
soft yellow daffodils
the tangle of wild geraniums
silently breaking ground
their budding faces and
tightly wound leaves
stretching toward life
as they claim their place
along my back wall

I feel the northern breeze nuzzle my neck
calling the river's dance
to its eastern shore
in whitecap formation
like the Rockettes across the stage

Today will not look like yesterday
nor like tomorrow
It's the day to fly my kite
let it pillow in the wind and lift
me into infinite space

where I can scribble my name
across the sacred sky
where penmanship doesn't count

Reincarnation

A billion light years before the moon
I rode the fiery arc of a comet's tail

spiraling through endless galaxies of velvet blackness
a glowing stellar cocoon within the void's dark cold.

Its atoms split into a million hot embers.
Blackness pulsed with heat and light

lingering until the white dwarf and butterflies
exploded and I became rainbows.

Now I write with colored inks of nebulas
waiting to split again to become the poet's pen.

About the Author

JP DiBlasi is a native New Yorker currently living and writing in the Hudson River town of Ossining. Her poems have appeared in four anthologies: *All the Women Came and Sang* (Wyld Side Press 2025); *From the Inside: NYC Through the Eyes of the Poets Who Live Here* (Blue Light Press, 2022); *Never Forgotten, 100 Poets Remember 9/11*, (North Sea Poetry Scene Press, 2022); and *Carrying the Branch: Poets in Search of Peace* (Glass Lyre Press, 2017). Her chapbook, *No Longer Gravity's Partner*, was published in 2019 by Blue Light Press. Other poems have appeared in: *Poetry Breakfast, RiverRiver, The Crazy Child Scribbler, Persimmon Tree*, and *Chronogram.*

JP is interested in traditional Irish music and attends local music sessions. She also teaches the bodhrán, the Irish goatskin drum. Friends love her sense of humor.